WAITING FOR
SASKATCHEWAN

WAITING FOR SASKATCHEWAN

FRED WAH

· TURNSTONE PRESS · 1985 ·

Published with the assistance of the Manitoba Arts Council and the Canada Council.

Turnstone Press
607-99 King Street
Winnipeg, Manitoba
Canada

Typeset by B/W Type Service Ltd. and printed by Hignell Printing Ltd. for Turnstone Press.

Printed in Canada.

First printing, 1985
Second printing, 1986
Third printing, 1987

Cover Design: Darlene Toews

Some of these poems have appeared, and several in slightly altered form, in *Breathin' My Name with a Sigh* (Talonbooks, © 1981 Fred Wah).

Canadian Cataloguing in Publication Data

Wah, Fred, 1939-
  Waiting for saskatchewan

Poems.
ISBN 0-88801-096-6

I. Title.
PS8545.A33W3 1985   C811'.54   C85-091382-9
PR9199.3.W33W3 1985

A Prefatory Note

Some of the poems from *Breathin' My Name With A Sigh*
were published in an edition of that text by Talonbooks in
1981. They are included in this book to give
some shape to the range of forms a particular content
("father") from that long poem has generated.

Grasp the Sparrow's Tail was privately published in a small
edition in Kyoto in 1982. It is a *utaniki*, a poetic diary
of mixed prose and poetry.

The *Elite* series explores further the tenuous division
between those two genres in working with the prose poem.

The final section of this book is a series of *haibun*, short
prose written from a haiku sensibility and, in this case,
concluded by an informal haiku line.

Such formal concerns have been at the heart of wonderful
conversations with bp Nichol, Robert Kroetsch, and many
other companions of the line. I'd like to thank them.

I'm also grateful for the support of a Canada Council arts
grant and a University of Manitoba writer-in-residence
appointment in 1982-83 when most of this book was
written.

June, 1985

CONTENTS

from Breathin' My Name With A Sigh

Waiting for saskatchewan
and the origins grandparents countries places converged
europe asia railroads carpenters nailed grain elevators
Swift Current my grandmother in her house
he built on the street
and him his cafes namely the "Elite" on Center
looked straight ahead Saskatchewan points to it
Erickson Wah Trimble houses train station tracks
arrowed into downtown fine clay dirt prairies wind waiting
for Saskatchewan to appear for me again over the edge
horses led to the huge sky the weight and colour of it
over the mountains as if the mass owed me such appearance
against the hard edge of it sits on my forehead
as the most political place I know these places these strips
laid beyond horizon for eyesight the city so I won't have to go
near it as origin town flatness appears later in my stomach why
why on earth would they land in such a place
mass of pleistocene
sediment plate wedge
arrow sky beak horizon still waiting for that
I want it back, wait in this snowblown winter night
for that latitude of itself its own largeness
my body to get complete
it still owes me, it does

Relation speaks. Tree talks hierarchy loop subject returns.
Knowledge a bag of things to be changed later to
knowledge. Statement of instructions horoscope Wah
language reads reading out of order in order to speak to
itself feed picked up lists family and complete branches/
worlds end there.

Are origins magnetic lines across an ocean
migrations of genetic spume or holes, dark
mysteries within which I carry further into the World
through blond and blue-eyed progeny father's fathers
clan name Wah from Canton east across the bridges
still or could it all be lateral craving hinted
in the bioplasmic cloud of simple other organism
as close as out under the apple tree?

Father, when you died you left me

with my own death. Until then I thought

nothing of it. Now I see it's clear cut

both genetic "bag" as well as choice. I know now

I'd better find that double edge between you

and your father so that the synchronous axe

keeps splitting whatever this is the weight of

I'm left holding.

my father hurt-
ing at the table
sitting hurting
at suppertime
deep inside very
far down inside
because I can't stand the ginger
in the beef and greens
he cooked for us tonight
and years later tonight
that look on his face
appears now on mine
my children
my food
their food
my father
their father
me mine
the father
very far
very very far
inside

just counted for his death I
cried once privately and once
public—7 years later

the father entwined
those bones brown (2 branches
or a towel twisted
to wring the water)

thought out empty
until I could count
on it. Him
and then me.

When you die it snows
late September mountain peaks

everytime it happens, I see it
and I think of you then

your sister Ethel
she says white is unlucky

it snowed today at timberline
it's never very far away is it

each year at first snow
your death makes more sense to me

father it is fall
the leaves turn
the hills
ready for winter again
the river and the town
cars parked along the streets
reflect the sunlight
movement is in holding
bodies with the years
I'm over forty now
they took down the Diamond Grill sign
mother took a trip to China

time
is an interference
with work
            music
has shape   (splitting birch this weekend)

father
again it is another season
the turning of it always
the spin
is sound
yet soundless at the core

to say this to you is nothing now
nothing
yet

breathing in the water so much story

to tell time times so simple rhythm

counting things like early snow mountain

peaks body skin with hair finger-

nails the death past 54 measure know

nothing rotten smell histories it like

layers of froth the scarlet letter parts

genital breathing lengths stretched

swimming swimming father's parts out

the grandfather father lineal
grampa's smile
your walk his
smile
the grampa eyes twinkle
yours serious
my shoulders
his watch
your ring
him thinking me ahead of him
my own self's others' know it
think "eight spot" and take
a chance

lineal
face, body's
things
a hemi-
sphere

IN THE ARMS OF THE FAMILY

IN THE ARMS

IN THE CENTRE OF THE ARMS

IN THE BODY

IN THE ARMS

OF THE FAMILY

IN THE ARMS OF MY FATHER

SKY

OF MOTHER NIGHT

IN THE ARMS OF US ALL OUR HOLDING

IN HIS/HER ARMS THEN

HIS MOTHER'S MY GRAND

FATHER'S

ARMS

your name is my name

our name is bones

bones alone names

left over slowly

to send signs forward

found out needed

knowing names

parts family imprint

left shape all over

us within it

name signed

me name

as our name

added-up knowns

become truths

said-again things

left over after

sedimentary hard

embedded rock to tell

getting at how the river in its mud banks flows downstream
contained mouth or breath fluid down to the toes outside
the house in the wind the dark and stormy brother's sister's
blood keep coming back into the word alongside itself a
bear and an angry man/woman family blood keeps it now
my daughters for the sky-clearing moon and men their own
river a cleft in the earth colour languaging a feeling inside
the surface tension from the breadth of my mother/father
things I am also left over thing put together calendar's event
reflexive world the children's things and wind last night/
biography

the first bridge was in Trail

and it crossed over the first river

full of fish and it moved with weight

not speed the first mountain

a hill of sand and scrub brush

Ernie's dog Mickey died

it's where Donnie was born

the Trail Smoke Eaters

were the World Champions

Brother   then brothers

number / age

"a matter

            of penetration"

the three of us

someday take that on

each one of us

older then

            than father

brothers

"got" his eyes, sister

after the brothers

genetic it, you

left

with your own fatherness

the way you gibe the men in your life

his dark, brown, taunting eyes

Caught looking. Throat thinking. Things feeling out the numbers when here and who sits later now and you look for it, open the door, or up by the creek, Cottonwood Creek, the sluice things remember terms how many not years except all those other things (items intact) exactly as yours or my years the branch off a maple for a new bow, twigs and arrows baseball "the" seasons memory of cousins in the Kootenay mountains numbers all stuck at the moment when the whole hillside town and lifetime work aunts and uncles grannies and grampas looking makes not sense simply colour touch surprise springs to the body caught looking throat thinking.

Your hands are so old. Numbers 43 23 82 looking ahead. Numbers out of every new year now you. Complete age. Held so often sitting beside you on a sofa, on a bus, on a beach, in a rowboat on a lake up the hill in the snow and the rain and the leaves. Hands so old. The "inging" of a life like an arrow. Flesh counts. Numbs our eyes and hair grows on our bodies year to year out of age only. We love us and us. Hands old.

The kids come home in the rain from a day in the car at
school music and all the things going on inside their heads
figure out a network for living to live in front of the voice
and talk to each other at the same time duplex model
modulate and play off the days around for seventy-five years.

Day tells you time of year except for not giving full sun or
bird but each day does explicit red-breasted robin, birch
tree apple branch and song light so image specific the
daughters in their new school dresses by the flowers on the
lawn morning mist try to mind the years later an actual
ocean day's daytime song, bird, etc.

Mood is the word out for release easy to pileup of pieces
skin deep empty of the heat welled up inside the body
imprint forward of the stomach's map to show last step
heard or left over from epoch or set prior to thing which
comes out of the whole person as he says like the sun.

"We never talk much we say to each other in the kitchen after work when the space there for our mouths needs to be filled. The silence all animals make to meet the same need. E. has come home from dancing, to a late supper. Lh. doesn't move from the warmth of the rocking chair near the stove. Real silence is usually freezing P. thinks (silently) to herself" he says.

Horse #1

Doing the horse and wait for the chi to rise to my tan t'ien
eyes levelled ten feet ahead on the floor world in front of
a mind which ravels (cradled) so in the body in the lake
fish fishing swim and float up the point stand and dance
then sit into the air imagining and think in a female line
of all the other things coming through

Horse #2

Horse within memory settled into spinal stance
Horse as father
   world national hierarchic memory of every other country
           every possible inhabitable body
   national
person   whole
Horses as in any of us   just standing
tight-assed pelvic cocked forward
arms to connect shoulders, feet, hooves, the boy's mind
              rational to expect the bit
   as a father too
   a whole political intention
             set
    too straight.

Horse #3

Horsing around yes with the invisible "tumbler" to carry
the map and move the eyes into cartographicness portaged
in minutes to the face of the sky seen as the horse "world"
stood there to do the sky to do the lakes around here as
"the plan" of the body will know ahead the head intellect
planning the game with horse narrative brought about as a
position no in the body going full horses of the intestinal
into the world here horse, around and around, yes.

Grasp The Sparrow's Tail
(a poetic diary)

You never did the "horse" like I do now but walked
straight down the aisle of the Diamond Grill
and kicked the kitchen door with such a slap
all the way up to the soda fountain
I know it's you.

You played "timber" with your eyes and voice
and laughed always as you fisted the coins
deep secret gabardine pocket jingle and sudden thrust
hard out on the arborite counter no chance
they try to get past your bluff.

You moved your body on the go even when you stood
head and shoulders arms too swing with the talk
rhythm to hardworking feet (I loved to shine
your alligator shoes, special, for going out only)
and then you died dancing.

July 28
In Vancouver just before trip to China and talk with G of
different ways the writing could get done. J's birthday.

Her a daughter's birthday think China book out linked to
poetry each day something new apparent each word capable
of total Chinese character baggage really gain sight of
word's imprint to pose itself as action on the world in the
context of the journey somewhere get ready for the Canton
poem

Aug 1
Over the Pacific between Honolulu and Japan. Dreamt last
night about a poem of me sitting on a bus-stop bench in
L.A. but of course I couldn't remember it this morning,
the poem that is. Just now while napping on the plane I
dreamt of the words I missed but even now I can't remember
them.

Thought of making part of book "the" Family can be known
by initial as in J and E and Lh but anyone else by full
name could mean group caste imprint exotic typology
genetic histories name language carries also later I get a
small bloodstone chop with schwa for my sign others choose
personal designs varietal identity, definition, red ink, lucky
green, a spot, either on the body or not

*The notes to what I could do rather than doing are always
like that, thinking it out ahead of time. Obviously I'm in
my mind too much and that enters dreamland too. But, I
say to myself, keep the ears open for possibilities and leads.
The two oriental languages on the plane are Korean and
Japanese.*

Japanese female language so light nearly a giggle or think
of R and his defiance the other night before we left now
grammar how to question verb over noun equals situation
picture how to staccato Japanese and something on colour
or pudeur in dream too or just before or after

Aug 2
Wake up in Kimi Ryokan after arriving during typhoon in
Tokyo last night. Had difficulty finding this place M had
told us about but from Ikebukuro station we had the help
of a Japanese college student. Walked through the Pachinko
neon and narrow back streets eyes wide, in the rain and
sweating with the heavy bags. This syntax, have to reverse
the English to fit, like

Tokyo
windy is
wind out in the ryokan courtyard
all night noise in the trees is

and think of different voices but I'm sore and tired this
morning from that adventure last night

The others' voices in their poems sharp, his and hers, PW's
clean b.p.'s narrative thought then in the calm of the writing
in the morning also the Tosa Diary and my own journey
the danger of focussing on the particular e.g. of the very
narrow stairs at Kimi stones set into the large hardwood
floorboards shine like tile the blueprint and architecture of
our six mat room here

Aug 3
Dreaming in Tokyo. The margins of the page, the limits the
"boundary walker" and Duncan's Shinto gate, the arche,
the architecture, the roof beam (?), prime, oriental ridge
pole. The buildings are low, not many skyscrapers as P
points out because of the earthquake possibility and she
reminds me of Frank Lloyd Wright's waiter with the tray
idea. Getting out of jet lag into "time" now. Thinking a
lot of sex, literal sensation. Plastic food in the windows
image for each meal. I like the narrow streets with all kinds
of small shops with the talk close like the long last night
stroll with P after a meal in the "O, O." Building

Orient last night before and after supper and remember
"information" with new "Sony Nude" plugs in ear stereo
surface to skin technology also the multi bright colours
and green sheen rooftop tiles futons hung flagged on
balconies for wind and sunny day and in a lineup her
clean flat and shining black hair in front of me is so far
away distant untouchable strange that should be

Aug 4
Get from Tokyo to Narita airport then to Seoul, Taipei
and Hong Kong. Now wait in airport transit lounge in
Taiwan for flight to continue. In Cantonese language
territory I feel more comfortable with an exhibit of beautiful
mainland calligraphy, painting and ceramics brought over
by Chiang. Western piano music. I watch a bald-headed
nun or monk and dark ethnic Chinese, maybe Tibetan.
P reads a novel by Patrick White, goof plot she says. Eyes
tired from what, body just tired.

Is that Chopin with the waxed evening light people me
looking so hard for something to connect with sounds or
faces an image out of all my images story unknown building
blocks from then to now tangent to hearing a rhythm
without having to pay attention to the melody?

Aug 5
We tour Hong Kong today in a bus with a guide hyping
photos of ourselves. I start taking notes re places I've seen
my father since he died. I think of him here in this city, in
transit, 60 years ago. See first statues and full of colour
(white is death, why Ethel didn't want a white coffin for
him, red for marriage) numbers too, 9 for longevity and
active life, 8 for wealth (there it is the 8-spot lottery
Grampa's gambling smile confirmed).

Numbers in everything said

    clatter each block commerce tooled

fronted with "making" some piece or all of it

    "lucre" personal contrivance shuttle

family woven decades ahead first

    his father and even him and his son

place attribute magnetic magic

    machined into tailored jade street single

attempt to move made so that "generation" gets

    skyline to 1997 after direct incant from

latitude Cantonese genocide nil hope stalled not

    to edit out immigrant identity cancel

head count not really meaningful money exchange

    added up with calculation mind counts the years

abacus clicks in the market stall can't wait

    for seasonal switch typhoon number late

afternoon maybe a winter somewhere in his mind

    but far away, far away.

Aug 8
In Canton (Guangzhou) now after train ride out from Hong
Kong. I see my father everywhere. I realize he was only
five years old when he arrived in China.

You would have had to learn Cantonese

just as you acquired Canadian prairie world view age 5.

Must have hurt to have to find new boyhood lingo

(so silence)

then at 19 to relearn English Swift Current

Elite Cafe sufficiency. What tax on your life

left you with all that angry language world inside

and from China too (silent)

There is all this tangibility to my life here, things I can
touch base with. I don't let myself feel "foreign" here, even
with my funky expectations of their political life which I
find so mysterious. I look at the red soldiers in the train
station with awe, and the workers in the streets become
some sort of generalization about themselves from the real
imagination, e.g. the streets are full of "masses." But the
person is what one aces so this is exactly where I should
pay attention to "ontogeny."

Don't let valour go with the name chiefly

in the accumulated value of the family a prize

within the state strength is bondless unless

the heart carries this calculated boldness outside

to exude many such indications about ourselves

such as the relative colour inside of me or inside of you.

So what have I got going besides this "father" list? I watched a painter leaned over the table doing calligraphy last night, watched him, watched his body, looked for his "chi" rising to the surface, quick, flashy, very intentional moves, so the flurry of the brush was true. I like the actualization of the intent which was not an intent an inclination, really, a bent or a "tropos" which was paid attention to. Me. I've misplaced the family information my mother gave me so I can't check out actual possible connections still here in the Canton region. I mention this to the guides and the others in our tour group, tell them my father was sent here as a child to be raised and educated by his Chinese relatives.

You were part Chinese I tell them.

They look at me. I'm pulling their leg.

So I'm Chinese too and that's why my name is Wah.

They don't really believe me. That's o.k.

When you're not "pure" you just make it up.

From Hong Kong on (to Guangzhou which used to be Canton, fly to Zhengzhou, then by train north to Taiyuan, Datong, and Huhhot and finally Beijing) I saw my father everywhere. Notes of these sightings resulted in the following prose extract.

About a year after you died I saw you. You were alone in a car and passed me going the other way. You didn't look at me. Over the past fifteen years this has happened maybe once or twice a year. I'll catch a glimpse of you on a street corner, disappearing through a doorway, or gesturing to someone in the booth of a Chinese cafe. What always gives you away is your haircut, your walk, or the flash in your eyes. You haven't seemed to notice me or ever said anything to me. In China your appearances were overwhelming.

One morning you were doing tai-chi in a park near our hotel in Kowloon. I saw the side of your head and the steadfastness of your face as you moved through the classic "Grasp the Sparrow's Tail." You wore a white sleeveless undershirt and khaki shorts, sandals, and your brush-cut was shorter than usual. It was quite early and very hot and humid. I watched you for a few minutes, from a distance. Your technique seemed forceful and you did your forms alone, out in the open.

After that I knew I would have some strong sensation of you in Canton. The very first morning on the street in front of our hotel I saw you riding your bicycle in the large crowd of bicycles which stream into town from the outskirts every morning. You had something in your mouth, scowl on your face, head down in private thought. Your face has always been very animated and usually says something. Later that same morning I caught a brief glimpse of you through the window of a roadside eatery gesticulating emotionally to someone across from you with your chopsticks. Your body still moves with emphasis and decision. I was quite excited about seeing you so frequently that day.

We visited a commune about 20 km outside Canton and I could imagine you and your sister Ethel working in the rice fields and living in this same small village when you were a boy. As I stepped into a courtyard I saw you ride by on a bicycle, again with a frown on your face. I could tell you were very concerned about something.

During the trip I saw you often and, curiously, moreso as we went north. Near the Yellow River you looked so relaxed as you leaned out the window of a truck being loaded with red bricks, enjoying your cigarette. I recognized your stocky frame as you bent to plant your fist of rice shoots in a field just outside Zhengzhou. Whether you were pushing your bike up a hill in the late afternoon in Taiyuan or walking briskly along the street in the coal-mining town of Shensi it was always your black crew-cut hair which most stood out.

Perhaps it was only the insinuation of youth from your ruddy cheeks but here in northern China you became younger and the redness of your complexion became more pronounced. To me you had always been older and now suddenly I was the older and watched you through this slick time-warp.

You are a father
I am a son and a father
and you were a son
so

I finally realized the full "truth" of these meetings at the Buddhist caves near Datong. There is a temple and a courtyard there, in front of the caves. I was about to leave and on a path alongside a wall you walked past me going the other way and brushed my arm. Yes, brushed. I could see it was intentional and our eyes met for an instant as you turned and glanced over the head of the baby boy you were carrying. Though you didn't say anything your face still talked to me.

Aug 10
Flying into Zhengzhou — stomach last night — turquoise on
C.A.A.C. Trident plane. Over rice paddies again — incessant
agriculture wherever possible — huge river plains —
symmetry of fields and irrigation channels — clouds — I
look for the voice — what has happened to colour — now
her voice comes over the P.A., about to land, etc. — the
9 tones of Cantonese the 4 tones of Mandarin.

When they plant the rice they bend their backs over and
fall into the sky of the water they look at all day long
look for extension out to other geographical scenes roots
and fist down in the mud dream of green large human
connection a terrain to give colour to the water and the
place table it

Friday Aug 13
In Taiyuan. Arrived yesterday after tiring all-night-long
train ride from Zhengzhou. Yakked late into the night with
the other men, some of their racist preconception seeping
in to take over the experience. Jumbled and noisy dreams
through the train tracks. I find the tour demanding physi-
cally as well so I haven't been doing much writing but
even this morning in the hotel I find the writing very
relaxing, dialogue set up with mind. I try the old-fashioned
pen nib and ink which is supplied in our room—stop to go
to the inkwell to get more ink with schooldays memory
synapse which allows the mind to gather the cloudhead of
thinking residue and push it out, every strand. The writing
during the day has no form or direction, just Father notes.
I've been reading Paul Engle's edition of Mao's poems,
good with lots of background notes, so I have some of that
floating around as I look, and look, and look.

The Answer to "Where is the official Tao Yuan-ming? in
Mao's poem "Ascent of Lu Mountain"

He's not plowing the field by Peach Blossom Spring.
It's August, the heat is too much
it shimmers the bushes,
and he, too, dreams of the oceans.
He's gone, took to the sky river like a father,
sells Laoshan mineral water late at night
on a train to Kokonee Glacier.

Aug 14
The caves at Datong were a central feature of our journey
and it is at about this time when the following prose-
poem was written.

You are me on a train going north through central China.
I don't think you've been here before; I haven't. You hold
out a green flag at the rear of the train. Then I see you
lounging on top of a pile of hemp rope on the station
platform and you look in through the train window, at me.
After the train starts to roll I watch you look out in quietude
at the countryside. As the sun sets over the loess hills you
look for remains of the Great Wall on the distant broken
ridges. There is a red star on your hat. Strangers come up
to you and ask questions in a foreign language. That lights
up your eyes. I think of the house you live in on the
Mongolian border with its south-facing door painted bright
yellows, oranges, and reds. You hardly ever think of that
door but the image is quickly accessible to you and when
you talk to a fellow-worker, a comrade, in your own
language, the colours of the door imbue your conversation.
As the train pulls into a station in the early evening
darkness you disappear.

A couple of days later, in the caves at Datong, you think
you recognize one of the statues, a bhodisatva with leg
bent at the knee. It reminds you of one of your parents
but you can't tell why or which one. Your parents, as you
remember them, have become one just as you were once
one in their married mind. An attempt to separate their
image into two separate people won't work. They are now

one in the image of this statue and this coalescence reminds
you of the singularity of origins, of the primary, the
fundamental, and that makes good sense to you, that
somewhere in this stone religion you would find something
of yourself. It is this very reflection of oneself in things
which accounts for you and I intersecting at this moment.
For example, the incredibly brilliant 800-year-old paint on
the statues here reminds you of lapis and the depth you
feel akin to in that rock, though I remember you were
always hot on jade, more cultural than personal I think.
As you sit in the warmth of the August morning sun and
write this you have attracted a large crowd of Chinese
who stop to watch the language flow out onto the paper.
You look up at them and ask them in English if they would
like to write something on your paper but they simply
smile and ignore you. They are more interested in the
writing and comment to one another and point to the
actual incisions you make on the paper, the calligraphy
of the foreign letters cutting also into their minds as they
recognize something of themselves there. When you think
about it all sorts of connections are lost.

Sometime later that day, on the hotel steps, you and I are
two old men smoking cigarettes and listening to the jarring
brass gongs of a Chinese opera on the radio. They just
look into one another's eyes. The gong usually signals a
movement on stage.

Monday, August 7
We travel all day out to the Inner Mongolian grasslands in
a small passenger van. Through the bus window I catch
yet another glimpse of "you."

You might have been this guy in Huhhot—one room, one
rooster—or is my skin bone brown so singular and
contained in China eyes deep within the common view
connected so that I see what you saw sometimes just to
stand in the doorway with creosote eyes imprint death
(too, maybe) but certainly to experience any complete
person living there is always a mirror how alone can one be?

In the late afternoon we arrive and I sit and look out of a yurt at the beautiful landscape of long, flat, rolling plateau and prairie horizon. A herd of camels brushes the camp and then moves faster than we can run into the distance. There's a lovely flush on the Mongolian girls' cheeks which is very attractive. Someone says it's from dairy products and outdoor living. I think of "pudeur."

The blush/flush shy guilt blood rush sign which is the origin of colour from the inner heat we rush outward (other animals don't blush do they?) these girls sing for us shrill voices behind the heat in their cheeks like in my family when they drink or the love of my daughters too in their first flush/first guilt so red something of the Scarlet Letter is why JC pointed to the story as the truth which rises from some depth sensation feeling the deep heat in the parts of the body move and make yourself so red which tells the story the tell-tale blush of revelation we are.

Tuesday
Raining this morning but now the sun is out. We visited a
yurt house and had some great yogurt. It's made straight
from milk without boiling; they leave fresh milk sit for 2-3
days so actually it becomes sour cream but this wasn't sour.
Too much riding on our bus through the countryside these
last few days. Images of our trip, the terrain, and P.

Hue of loess August terrace planted green and heavy water
then yellow dry by mid-September our marriage wanders
again through the millenia of marriages here in the earth
brush your knee on the bus, think of the caves, the yolk
of an egg, the rice.

Friday the 20th August in Beijing
Touring the city. Lotus fields everywhere. Look at the hats
they wear. Everything happiness and longevity.

At the Summer Palace the peach

the symbol of "lucre"

each picture different

from the classics

5,000 — no repetition

Or everywhere, the masses, the people from New York
airing their teeth. I think to try to get to the particular,
the minute, underneath the lushness of the ornamental, the
specific (therefore simple?), rediscover "decoration" as
useful, function.

The words for the things
    are not the things themselves
    of course

Mao's mausoleum, now the Great Hall of the People.
When we walked into the large room just before seeing
his body I was struck by the very large painting of the
mountains along one wall because of a poem I had written
years ago as I looked out over the mountains along the
Kootenay River from our house.

Mao, in front of me
the things you cared for too

river, mountain
a town, the whole
blue sky.

Elite
(pronounced ee-light)

Elite 1

Swift Current Saskatchewan is at the centre. I don't think
you were a boy there. Probably what happened is your
family moved there from Medicine Hat just before you
were four, just before you and Ethel were sent to China.
I know all these "facts" existed once, and I could check
some of them out with Ethel, or your other sisters and
brothers, Buster, Lil, Flo, Jimmy. But, like the information
on distant relatives I lost just before going into China,
somehow I don't want it or don't need it. The facts seem
partially unreal. Anyway, you must have seen Swift Cur-
rent just before Grampa put you on the train. About
1923. I was driving across the prairies on New Year's
eve last year and we decided to stop for the night in
Swift Current. It was close to midnight and so we thought
we'd welcome in the New Year in a pub downtown. I
hadn't been there for over thirty years but I felt natural
in following Central Ave. to the old train station. As
soon as I saw the station I knew exactly where I was. I
stopped the car and pointed out to Pauline the exact spot
I stood when the war was over and I met you at the
station when you came home from training camp. From
there the lay of the land was clear to me. There was
Roy's shoe shop and just up the street across from Wool-
worth's was the Elite Cafe. You were always there, in the
Elite, working. I remember the streets more on my own.
Not just the photographs, but me walking, alone in the
town. Touching a building, the flowerpots in Mother
Trimble's windowsills, the cool shade under some outside
stairway, etc. I never talked to you about these things,
even when they weren't memories. They weren't really

important at the time. Your memory of such particulars. Mine. Does it matter? The reason for the story is simply to count on it. What I remember or what you or anyone else connected remembers isn't the point. There isn't even any point. There is just this. You, before you had a car, on the street in an overcoat, winter, to work. Always alone. I mean I see only your singularity, you with hands in your pockets, head down, going to work, with intention, in the cold winter dusk, to the Elite, your dad or Buster already has the big stainless coffee urn ready, what was it, twenty cups of ground in the cloth sack and, what, the first few customers, not farmers, you can't even speak English at first, silence, from China too, sweep the floors, maybe do some cooking in the kitchen where you can talk to the cooks, Grampa out front flipping coins, the whole family around you there in Swift Current, your new old family, by then silence and anger hum, alone.

Elite 2

Do you remember how living on the prairies was like living in water, in an ocean or a large lake. Movements, decisions, fortunes were made by undercurrent, a sense of sliding along a large floor, in the night. The night I was with you on a trip, just before we moved out to B.C., it felt like that, the way we moved, probably by train, through unknown territory. Always you had an "intent." You were on business of some sort and the others we met were all Chinese. You could talk to them. They gave me candy and pinched me. You and they talked and talked. Chinese always sounds so serious, emotional, angry. I napped on a couch in some Chinese store in some Alberta town. The old men played dominoes and smoked and drank tea. In the window dusty plants in porcelain bowls and some goldfish. Does it seem strange to you now to see this in words? Do you remember the trip I'm talking about? Late at night somewhere you played Mah Jong. From outside the sound of the click-clack of the pieces being shuffled over the tabletop under the hum of the men's voices, a real music I felt comfortable with. Even though you stayed late you always came back, going somewhere. We moved that night through this subcontinent of prairie landscape, it was summer and the water was warm and hazy, the possible distances, distant.

Elite 3

I'm on the prairies this winter. I haven't been here in the winter since I was four years old. It's not Swift Current, or Speedy Creek as some here call it, but there are certain flavours which are unmistakeably part of us. The ethnicity here feels so direct. I mean the Chinese are still connected to China, the Ukrainians so Ukrainian, in the bar the Icelanders tell stories about Iceland, the Swede still has an accent, the French speak French. Here you're either a Wiebe or a Friesen, or not. What is a Metis, anyway? I know when you came back from China you must have felt more Chinese than anything else. But I remember you saying later that the Chinese didn't trust you and the English didn't trust you. You were a half-breed, Eurasian. I remember feeling the possibility of that word "Eurasian" for myself when I first read it in my own troubled adolescence. I don't think you ever felt the relief of that exotic identity though. In North America white is still the standard and you were never white enough. But you weren't pure enough for the Chinese either. You never knew the full comradeship of an ethnic community. So you felt single, outside, though you played the game as we all must. To be a mix here on the prairies is still noticed. I remember going into Macleods in Swift Current a few years ago and sensing that most of the women in the store were just like Granny Erickson. I don't think you felt there was anyone else in the world like you.

Elite 4

You got us involved in the Salvation Army because that's what Granny Wah wanted. She had a bonnet. I can't recall ever seeing Grampa or you there. But I bet she had her go at you too. Didn't you ever play the big bass drum, or the cymbals? I played the E-flat horn later in Nelson. I think, like Grampa, you always thought the Salvation Army people outside yourself. That was the Chinese in you. You didn't outwardly really trust it. But you tried it. In some totally pure and personal way you prayed, alone. I know later when our family went to the United Church in Nelson and you sometimes got off work on Sunday morning to go to church with us you did sing the hymns but your brow furled as if you couldn't understand the words. You were proud, then, of the fact you were going to church and you made a point of telling some of the customers in the restaurant that you had to go to church. That was after you had stopped desiring China and the Chinese at work put up with but laughed at you going to church. I think the church thing was white respectability and you did it for that and a sense of our family in that community. Somehow in the face of all the Salvation Army, Granny, community, etc. I know you established some real spiritual communication, totally private, no drums.

Elite 5

There is no picture (or is there) of me leaning over the boards of the Swift Current arena with you there, on the ice in your big overcoat, suit and tie, spiffy, smiling at the camera, and the whole Swift Current Indians (they weren't real "indians"—that was their name) hockey team working out, swirling big as life over the dark ice. There is a team picture I know. Like the Toronto Maple Leaf hockey calendars that used to hang in the barber shop, the team lined up on the real ice of the Gardens against the backboards. But in this one it's the Indians. I think you were the manager or something, you helped out. The brim of your hat is turned down, Chicago gangster style. The Indian on their sweaters is just like the Chicago Black Hawks. Strangely, Chicago figured in your life. You told us that you ran away from home when they brought you back from China and got work on a boat in the Great Lakes. You jumped ship in Chicago and they picked you up for illegal entry. You were sent back to Swift Current and that was the end of that. I wish you had given us more details. Chicago has always been a mysterious place for me and someday I'll get there myself. Anyway, isn't it strange how that city is there in our lives, on the periphery.

I've always been "proud" you were part of that team. The Swift Current Indians were my first hockey heroes and their movements over the ice instilled a sense of body and mind-set which I have carried with me all my life. Even though you never played hockey I know you had the invisible movement of the game inside you too. You said you played basketball on a winning team in China. But you liked hockey. There is no picture either of me and my first pair of skates, double-runners, with Mom (you were working), on a blustery day, natural ice, on a pond or creek. Or the skating rink you made for us in our back yard in Trail. Or the puck that caught me just above the eye, third row as you and I watched a game in the Civic Centre, blood and stitches. The game on television now, you'd fall asleep before the end of the first period. Did you ever ride a horse?

Elite 6

Line going deep into the lake or flung out onto the surface glaze river current, layers of darkness, invisible fish. You would look at me with serious brown eyes sometimes like I was crazy when I caught a fish and then give your own mad laugh. Something got to you fishing in the Columbia River at Trail, after work, along the rocks, swift-flowing mind emptying, maybe. Or in a creek at Meadow on a Sunday afternoon picnic, cousins and uncles, a ball game. At Apex you driving the road in the turquoise Ford looking for us fishing along the slow meandering of Cottonwood Creek. You without me at Trout Lake. Me without you below the C.P.R. tracks below Granite Road on the way out of town or jigging for suckers near the boathouses with the old Chinaman. When I fish now sometimes I feel like I'm you, water, glassy gaze, vertical, invisible layers, the line, disappearing.

Elite 7

The dream "noises" of the early morning. You getting ready to go to work, still dark at 4:30, a light dust of snow maybe, the house warm, as you dress, the gabardine pants, shoes I shined for you last night, muffled voices of goodbye, the small change in your pocket, car keys, your pace on the varnished maple floor, alone, quickens with movement towards the door, out, dark grey mist-hackle across the lake on Elephant Mountain, you and the town get going for the day, I hear the blue 2-door Pontiac hum alive down on the street, and you're gone to work, and then our own half-awake silence and relaxation back into the morning's warmth and sleep. Or me a couple times a year getting up for you, e.g. father's day, some Sunday morning, could you really sleep "in" thinking of me the kid making the big urn of coffee, turning the heat up, remembering to get the cream and a tray of butter out of the cooler, turn on the sign, the synchromesh of everything starting to work, darkness breaking on Baker Street, first customers and the regulars early morning old man risers C.P.R. night shift and a few foremen and loners first coffee and cigarettes, the new noises of the day picking up speed and humming along the counter and booths to the whack of the kitchen door kicked on stride and the "smells" then.

Elite 8

I try to "place" you and the hand or head can't, try to get you into my mountains for example but your China youth and the images of place for you before you were twenty are imbued with the green around Canton rice fields, humid Hong Kong masses—I can't imagine what your image of the world was, where you were in it (were you always going home to Swift Current, were you ever at home, anywhere). How much did you share of how small or large the world was after we left the prairies—Trail, Nelson, Cranbrook, Calgary, Vancouver? That "reward" of a real holiday down the Columbia and then up the coast to Vancouver when you sold a share in the Diamond Grill. A few trips to Spokane, hikes into the hills around Nelson for fishing, the gravelly drive to Trail and back. Did any shape of such places ever displace the distancing in your eyes? You looked out at it all but you never really cared if you were there or elsewhere. I think you were prepared to be anywhere. The sun, the warmth, was something you went outside for, outside yourself, stretching and relaxing your working moving body, inside, inside, you never betrayed any imprint of a "world" other than your dark brown eyes.

Elite 9

When you returned from China via Victoria on Hong Kong Island and they put you in jail in Victoria on Vancouver Island because your birth certificate had been lost in the Medicine Hat City Hall fire and your parents couldn't prove you were born in Canada until they found your baptism records in the church or in the spring of 1948 when we moved to Nelson from Trail during the floods while Mao chased Chiang Kai-shek from the mainland to offshore Taiwan and the Generalissimo's picture hung in our house and on a wall above some plants and goldfish in the Chinese Nationalist League house down on Lake Street or when you arrived in China in 1916 only four years old unable to speak Chinese and later in the roaring twenties when each time Grampa gambled away your boat passage so you didn't get back to Canada until 1930 languageless again with anger locked up in the immigration cells on Juan de Fuca Strait or when your heart crashed so young at 54 as you fell from mom's arms to the dance floor did you see islands?

Elite 10

Your father owned the Regal across from the railway station but you worked in the Elite on Central Avenue right next to the Venice and the Paris was the one on the corner all three across the street from Cooper's store where Connie worked in the dry goods department after school and then full time after graduation the year you took her to the final basketball game at Gull Lake and Mom says now you borrowed a car and drove to Moose Jaw for a honeymoon and bought your first house in Swift Current in the fall of 1939 for $900 just after I was born and Connie's Dad fixed it up so you sold it and bought another, stucco (I remember that one) in '41 then moved to Trail in the spring of '43 and bought the Expert Cleaners and sold it to Andy's brother Sam and his wife and bought a house there on a corner right across from the river near Butler ball park by the bridge and the next one where we had our first dog it was down closer to Sandy Beach where Granny and Grampa lived at the foot of Sandy Mountain and then Ernie's dog Mickey up in the house in the next block to the Dollar Cleaners all in East Trail while you and Grampa were in the Elite across the river downtown underneath the smelter hill and then in the spring of '48 floods when we moved to Nelson didn't you and Jimmy Gee Ethel's husband buy into the L.D. Cafe which you changed to the New Star just as Mao's victory north of the Yangze became palpable and we lived in the duplex with the oil stove at 314 Carbonate before you got into your last restaurant (and mine) the Diamond Grill which even with the Standard down by Hipperson's Hardware times got good on Baker Street in the fifties and you got Grampa Erickson to build us our own house with maple floors at 724 Victoria you were so proud we had fireworks for the house warming and two sittings for the Chinese banquet in the basement and finally the Holmes Motel in Cranbrook in the early sixties where that was the end of the deals the cafes the houses the driving the building the running right through it, for you, that was it.

This Dendrite Map:
Father/Mother Haibun

Father/Mother Haibun #1

Finally changed the calendar today to August. Sitting here
this morning trying to figure out things (phone rings and
she asks "Is this David? I must have the wrong number. I
don't know why I keep doing this.") the *ecrit* I'm open for,
ungular, now alone in the mornings looking through Jung
and Hillman for hints, I mean the simple and solid clarity
of my father's father's dying, his dying, and then me living
and then dying too is outrageous, bald as geographical
Saskatchewan and my Grandfather which made my life
"racial" not that he actually came to be there but simply
him here/there and her, my Grandmother, her Salvation
Army Englishness really solid in the middle of his flux but
both of them cutting "geo" out of their world thus Maple
Creek Moose Jaw North Battleford Medicine Hat somewhere
in England and Canton China places in their lives much
more than in their world, you, my father, almost too,
thus me, such particles caught in the twig-jam holding
the water back impedimenta and this dendrite map I'm
finally on now for no reason but time, and then I'll go to
the city and look for an S-shaped chair to hold me and
this up.

Two weeks late I turn the calendar, crave for ripe tomatoes

Father/Mother Haibun #2

Anger the same thing as you behind my face, eyes, maybe.
A larger than usual black bear, eating, high up in the thin
wild cherry trees in the gulley this morning, sun just coming
up. I peer around the corner of the garage at the bear just
like you would, eyes squinted brow lined in suspicion like
yours used to, as if you were trying to figure out something
serious. I feel your face in me like that sometimes, looking
out of me, and now I wonder if my anger is the same as
yours flying out of me from him and his, etc. the anger
molten back through Cthonic fear. The bear flushed off,
finally, by the dog. You hover in the cool August morning
air, behind my eyes. The fire, the candle, the pumpkin,
the "virtu," inside.

Crash of broken branch, hungry, pits in the shit

Father/Mother Haibun #3

I try talking to you in this near-September air after I water
the dry spots out of the lawn, morning sunny and clear
the air coming to this for months ahead, almost, your
death-month, turning the flowers, even those huckleberries
I picked yesterday had thoughts of the frost ahead high in
the mountains, such simple weather but something more
primitive here pictures of the kids each year on the first day
of school in front of the flowers in their new clothes, ahead,
you too and my mind working over the connections, you're
laughing, sceptical, like when I told you they used hot
water to make the ice at the arena because it steams and
you just about believed it because I did, my heart shoots
into the memory of that actual mouths-and-eyes-talking
dialogue, weather is memory every time I wonder if you
ever really listened to the songs on the Wurlitzer in the
cafe, particularly on a quiet winter Sunday afternoon, the
words anytime your mind roaming ahead and behind like
mine the little shots at living each day all the things air
carries for thinking like that.

**Music, I try to think of the words to Autumn Leaves, Love
Letters in the Sand**

Father/Mother Haibun #4

Your pen wrote Chinese and your name in a smooth swoop
with flourish and style, I can hardly read my own tight
scrawl, could you write anything else, I know you could
read, nose in the air and lick your finger to turn the large
newspaper page pensively in the last seat of those half-
circle arborite counters in the Diamond Grill, your glass
case bulging your shirt pocket with that expensive pen,
always a favourite thing to handle the way you treated it
like jewellry, actually it was a matched pen and pencil set,
Shaeffer maybe (something to do with Calgary here), heavy,
silver, black, gold nib, the precision I wanted also in things,
that time I conned you into paying for a fountain pen I
had my eye on in Benwell's stationery store four dollars
and twenty cents Mom was mad but you understood such
desires in your cheeks relaxed when you worked signing
checks and doing the books in the back room of the cafe
late at night or how the pen worked perfectly with your
quick body as you'd flourish off a check during a busy
noon-hour rush the sun and noise of the town and the cafe
flashing.

**High muck-a-muck's gold-toothed clicks ink mark red green
on lottery blotting paper, 8-spot (click, click)**

Father/Mother Haibun #5

You can't drive through a rainbow I said hills to myself in the mountains glory of a late summer early fall thunder storm the Brilliant Bluffs brilliant indeed the shine rain and sunshine waves of science breaking lickety split school systems memory for the next word after colour from the other side no one could see it otherwise nature's path is home to the bluebird triangular son/event/father w/ time-space China rainbow over your youth vertical like on the prairies that rainbow stood straight up into the sky on the horizon you'd think in the winter sun ice crystals could form unbelievable

Radio on, up north an American hunter shoots a rare white moose, geese in the sky, nibbling ribbons

Father/Mother Haibun #6

I wish you were alive here in my life so we could share
the ease of our lives growing older together, now time
would catch up with the gap of our ages, 45-72, ethnicity
would be gone, just skin and the winding down, the fence
Jenefer & I built along the back, hockey games, the sunny
fall day, this sentimentalism, songs too, like crazy white
American juke box "Mule Train" in your imagination I
thought just as those events are in mine, no, but you and
the Great Lakes boats desire, absolutely your own, undying
care for the single, your own world fact, all this buffer,
as down the road in the village from us this so-called
community, the ones we care for really spread over the
whole earth if possible, padding of the family too, this
softness around ourselves so that we want it, so common
we could talk about it now, but so alone, so alone.

**I'll stain the fence red, a dim border in the snow, might
last thirty years**

Father/Mother Haibun #7

I was back in Buffalo when you died and when I came out
for your funeral at the end of September there was snow
on Elephant Mountain as far down as Pulpit Rock from
Ernie's house the lake quiet my mother alone suddenly,
months unused, unusual, I knew you best in the winter
when there was curling and hockey or in the summer when
we fished, dark mornings on the way to work or wet leaves
in the gutter, driving at this time of year from Cranbrook
to Nelson for the Lion's dance, car heater toasty warm
upholstery, outside the air wet and cool mist hackles in
the mountains your life simply closing down in the quiet
month on the Hume Hotel ballroom floor wobble of the
planet's sun seasons shortened golden flower's corny harvest
elixir completed.

Road's nearly empty, only a few pickups with firewood

Father/Mother Haibun #8

The pulse. So. When I take it now the microsystem wild card is almost cellular in its transport of the image imprint forward or I think back pictures. Some Saturday afternoons I'd have to take off work at the Diamond to play soccer down at the Civic, or you'd feed me a steak before a midget hockey bus trip to Trail, after the game Frenchie's french fries outside the Cominco, my earth my world which grosses more sensation, you knew more than I did, now my daughter has grown up into her stomach too, large encryptic sublease a full-grown symptom of I'm just curious about this body. You read it all, playing games is really not such a big deal but I always thought I had to pad it a bit to get off work, the world and out the door down the street, you knew it and me, outside the sun and the chemicals it's either numbers or that large front swinging wooden door.

Felled tree in the fall, I look at the stump for sap, zero

Father/Mother Haibun #9

"Why do you think of your father so much?"

"He's dead. Every once in a while I think I see him, or someone I see reminds me of him, or I'm writing this book and he's in it."

"That's not the truth. There's more to it than that."

"What we'll try for is a paradigm in this."

"You can think of a fishing cause. For him environment is connected with the earth."

"Dante phoned last night. From Salmo. And the day before, Mike Zoll showed up and told me 'The subtle quality of things transcends all formal boundaries.' I don't know, I'm not sure, maybe."

"Do women think a circle is a labyrinth?"

"Kore, no one wears purple like you. I half expect you to come with a hat."

"I feel I'm lucky I'm part Chinese when I see a river."

"So. What about your father?"

"Look, it's an old problem. When Smaro says 'Alley Alley Home Free' I know exactly what's going on. Her eyes twinkle. Here, it's snowing today. Sounds are deadened, like waking up in a room with the windows closed. Why do you ask?"

"*Autumn in New York, Moonlight in Vermont*, they're all haiku. And that's just one of the tricks Lionel knows. You know that poem about his dad and the echo of the axe on the other side of the valley? That was in the fall, there was frost. Or Victor's poem, 'Kenkyusha: Day Nine,' his daughter's birth, my father's death, zooming in on the phoneme of time, accurate, and asks me 'what time.'"

"You'd better ask Peter about Jack Clarke's Hegel's 'discipline of service and obedience' and 'the lake Fred Wah said it all ends up in' in case McNaughton and the hidden 'd' can help."

"Maybe tomorrow. I've been carrying it around all week. It's the epitaph to my Aunt Hannah's grave in Swift Current. It's like a song. Whenever I think of it I can hear my Granny Wah singing, front row, in the Salvation Army hall, and I can see her grey-blue eyes softened with a bit of surprise."

Hannah Elizabeth
fell asleep in Jesus Arms
1918-1936

Father/Mother Haibun #10

Working with my back to the window for more natural
light, dog chasing cows in the field, the words stubble
today, embedded there in the bracken at the edge of the
field, Chinese philosophy and numbers, the cloud-filled
night, "and they swam and they swam, right over the dam,"
etc., all this, and sugar too, holding the hook, time, the
bag, the book, the shape, you also carried on your back
yin and embraced yang with your arms and shoulders, the
mind as a polished mirror, there, back into my hand.

[handwritten: Chinese culture confuses him]

[handwritten: feminine as burden / masculine as useful]

**I can't stop looking at the field of brown grass and weed
and feeling the grey sky**

Father/Mother Haibun #11

Mother somewhere you flying over me with love and close
careless caress from Sweden your soft smooth creme skin
only thoughts from your mother without comparison the
lightness of your life/blood womaness which is mine despite
language across foetalness what gods of northern europe
bring out of this sentence we say and live in outside of
the wife of the storm god's frictive battle with the "story"
our names

**Rain washes first snow, old words here on the notepad,
"Where did Odysseus go?"**

Father/Mother Haibun #12

Mom you'll know this as a wordgame, strategy to get truth's
attention, your name, Corrine, for example, core, cortex,
heart, blood, islands of the liver, a tension to incite the
present, your friend Woody written into the texture,
coloured uphill under their apple tree beautiful also, we
were about fifteen when Wayne Waters said to me "Your
mother's a good looking woman" and I blushed, tissue of
skin, shades of other people's hair, touch.

**The landscape is red, "pudeur," an air of sanctity and
respect, etc.**

Father/Mother Haibun #13

The issue is to divide into two, duplicate, derive language
which is a filter for the blood, and then to replenish thought
in a precise flow to converge again on life, how much a
copy of you I am also a material for my own initials
(F.J.) Karen Marie Erickson when your mother died all the
undoubling condensed memory added up to a single snowy
winter month like January. *individuality? or just a combinatn*
of the parts?

**I get up and look, no sky today, just the fog. How one
can one be?**

Father/Mother Haibun #14

When my hands, arms, and head grew larger there was
at one point a very comforting sensation which I thought
might relate to my birth and you're constantly rubbing
your wrist joints this spherical map of "influence" as in
Dad's anger, maybe, or your clearing your throat. I wait
for simply old age and a mental space serrated description
narrative the same refrain female song a flair for the fictive
or theory that there is invocation in the inheritance of the
blue-print.

**In winter ravens look more majestic, weaving over the
highway, tree to tree, tree to tree**

Father/Mother Haibun #15

All this imaging is only the subliminal daily cache because
of your first real house and the "Just Mary" show *time*
with you in the radio air of the room carpet *Journeys
Through Bookland* "Tom and the Waterbabies" with story
every morning and on Sunday afternoons got "serial" eyes
with "Jake and the Kid" or John Drainey's story hour quiet
spring evenings Sgt. Drake on the Vancouver waterfront
breathing radio world innuendo a mother with secrets when
the snow blows in circles over the farms final connections
to the ancient world.   *—connections between new culture &
ancient world*

**Someday I'll grow them, prairie hollyhocks again, on a
stucco wall**

90

Father/Mother Haibun #16

I know the language just turns you into metaphor, rock of
ages like Granny Wah, the truth. Traces of the other
mothers, cliff-dwellers in the golden city, your windows
nothingnesses to the world's something, bisons on the walls
at Lascaux. So there. How to defend you and I from a
language edited by Christians I stand facing west with my
father and speak words which are new names for the sea.

*- learning Chinese culture despite endless barriers
constructed by western culture*

**Old month's countenance, deer swim the rock-wall river,
mean anything to you?**

Father/Mother Haibun #17

Oh Mother, the brightness of the birch tree's bark in this
November mid-afternoon sunset, fringes, the datum which
is permanent, the external events of all that stuff actual
energy is created from, you on a different planar syntax
Jenefer discovers in turning the yin/yang key, a cyclic
thing going on there, ontologic principle, all the daughters
want it, one pot, this morning I watered your Christmas
cactus bursting brilliant pink and purple on schedule for
your birthday again, and you should see Helen's, what'd
those philosophers say, he beats the drum, he stops, he
sobs, he sings, they had mothers. *Modern men's movement*

**You flew over me, outside there was a moist loss, now I
remember**

Father/Mother Haibun #18

I'd say that's a "proud" or swollen wound on my finger,
body's pride reminding itself of itself, something genitive
about the blue sloped roof of the '51 Pontiac, lives broken
into car eras both of you (thus us) the heat on the edge
of healing skin red something (eucharistical) and my own
two daughters even this spring, fall leeched ground and
then outside the flowers see how hard it is for me to make
sense of a hunch, looking around myself, looking for the
simple "of" connection might be, and why my friend Albert
set out his amaryllis this spring.

**No more snow to shovel this winter, back to the ground,
flowers**

Father/Mother Haibun #19

I'm here alone for the weekend, get fires going and burn
all that junk, mind keeps that there to clean up. I get some
rice on and the cabin's warm. Now I sit here sip a beer
and dwell on my aloneness, the solitary singleness and
being older now. That is a prediction I gave myself when
I watched some of the old men around town, isolation.
Night falling. Cold over the lake, fingers of clouds in the
western sky above Woodbury Creek. I told Peter that's the
process I'm interested in as long as I can keep getting the
language out. Now I'm as old as you were. The fire outside
in the dark comes from your eyes. The words of our name
settle down with everything else on this shore.

Smoke sits on the lake, frost tonight, eyes thinking

Father/Mother Haibun #20

I still don't know how to use the chopsticks as right or as
natural, bamboo fingers hands arms mind stomach, food
steaming off the dishes, rain or wet snow, windows, night
lights, small meals you'd grab between rushes (unlike me),
that's what you did, isn't it, went back to the cafe later,
on the nights we didn't have rice at home, me too, when
I first went to university in Vancouver I couldn't stand it,
I'd need rice, catch the Hastings bus to Chinatown, what
is it, this food business, this hovering over ourselves? *— connected to culture through father but not completely; not as much as would like*

**A little ginger, a little garlic, black beans, lo bok, Aunty
Ethel, the kitchen**

Father/Mother Haibun #21

Speedy dancing and the leaves of Germany meet me at the
elevator, words mean everything, I try to phone you on
mother's day, everyone does, more Swedish than Chinese,
you didn't want me to be a boy scout all my life, did you
(the leaves cling to this writing), sometimes to be battle-
ready Norbert Ruebsaat, genetics and geographies, he can
tell you too, exactly like mother alphabet the new lyric
feet, McKinnon's South America eyesight I tell myself my
self-perception, palace/place/police, spring leafless trees
on Ontario's horizon, did Pindar catch us dead in our
tracks?

**Japanese plum blossoms, my finger joints swollen, your
kind of love sweetest, get that, sweetest**